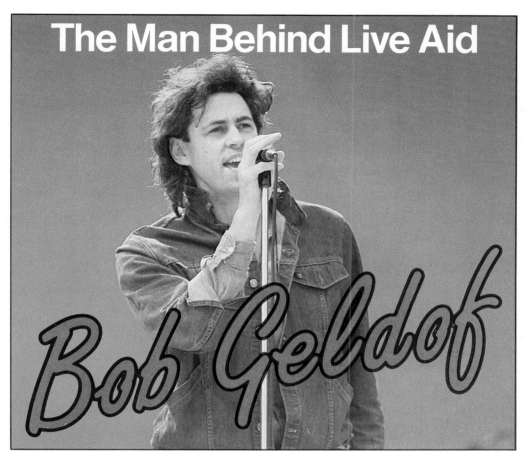

The Man Behind Live Aid

Bob Geldof

Nathan Aaseng

Lerner Publications Company
Minneapolis

LIBRARY OF CONGRESS CATALOGING-IN-PUBLICATION DATA

Aaseng, Nathan.
   Bob Geldof, the man behind Live Aid.

   Summary: Describes the early life, career, and
charity work of the Irish singer-songwriter, whose
musical achievements went relatively unrecognized until
he organized the Live Aid project to raise money for
famine victims.
   1. Geldof, Bob, 1952-   . 2. Live Aid (Fund
raising enterprise) — Juvenile literature. 3. Rock
musicians — England — Biography — Juvenile literature.
[1. Geldof, Bob, 1952-   . 2. Musicians. 3. Live
Aid (Fund raising enterprise)] I. Title.
ML3930.G27A63   1986   784.5′4′00924[B]   86-10597
ISBN 0-8225-1613-6 (lib. bdg.)

   1   2   3   4   5   6   7   8   9   10   96   95   94   93   92   91   90   89   88   87   86

Contents

The Most Famous Singer You've Never Heard

In 1984 someone destroyed the idea that the world's problems are far too large for an individual to make any difference. That person, a thirty-two-year-old Irishman, was described by a government official in Great Britain as having "done more to save the lives of famine-stricken people than anyone in history." For years he has been considered by some to be "the best lead singer that you never heard of." Now he has become the most famous and important modern musician whom you've never heard perform. His name is Bob Geldof and his band is the Boomtown Rats.

He was responsible for getting all the big stars to "check their egos in at the door" and join together to record "Do They Know It's Christmas?" and "We Are The World." He was the mastermind behind the incredible Live Aid concert that massed more than fifty of the top music acts in the world and beamed a sixteen-hour concert to an estimated one and a half billion viewers. Even Prince Charles and Princess Diana had to take a back seat at the Live Aid concert in London. Fans reserved their most thunderous applause for Bob Geldof.

Geldof's efforts to relieve a severe African famine have been so astounding that he has been nicknamed "St. Bob" by the British press. Bob has even been nominated by a member of the Norwegian parliament for the Nobel Peace Prize. Yet he is hardly the type of person you would expect to be put in the company of such past Nobel Prize winners as Albert Schweitzer, Martin Luther King, and Mother Teresa. In fact, Bob Geldof may be one of the last people parents would have wanted their children looking up to. His own friends say that he is sloppy, dirty, and a slob, that he has an ego the size of the Grand Canyon, and that he can strike up a heated argument with total strangers. Almost everyone agrees that Geldof can be loud and obnoxious, has little politeness or tact, that he constantly uses language that isn't fit for a family newspaper, that he rubs people the wrong way, that he has no patience, and that his lifestyle is looser than most people can tolerate.

This is the thoughtful side of Geldof, the side that strangers trust with their donations.

Yet this man inspires the kind of trust that even the most respected charities can only dream of. People who would ordinarily pass on by any hitchhiker who looked like Bob does, with his long, brown hair, ragged work shirt and faded jeans, walk up to Geldof with tears in their eyes and stuff wads of money into his hands. On one short airplane flight, Geldof's pockets were lined with the money of four different countries from people who had recognized him and wanted to contribute to his cause. There wasn't a doubt in their minds that every penny of it would go directly to famine relief.

How did this unlikely character succeed in raising the music industry to new heights and in outdoing the governments of the world in providing relief to Africa?

A Struggling Irish Rat

Surviving by his wits and his persistence, Bob Geldof has managed to blaze his own unusual path through both the music world and the maze of government regulations. It's the only way he has ever known how to live. Although he was born in 1952 into a reasonably ordered, middle-class home in Dublin, Ireland, that world quickly fell apart. Bob's mother died when he was six, and his father had to spend most of his working hours on the road. That left Bob, the youngest of the family's three children, at home alone most of the time. With no one to supervise him, Bob was forced to depend on himself.

School held no interest for him. Never having had much practice conforming to strict rules, Geldof rebelled whenever authority stood in his way. Bob was an odd combination of shyness and gab. He found it difficult to talk to girls, yet would argue the ears off anyone who disagreed with him. It didn't help when his classmates started teasing him about his appearance, and calling him "Rubber Lips." Fortunately, the full-lipped rock star Mick Jagger was bursting into fame during Bob's youth, and Jagger's popularity saved Bob a lot of grief.

Geldof's habit of speaking his mind on any subject drew him naturally into politics. He went along on a few marches and nuclear protests, but there was nothing the restless Geldof wanted to get tied down to. In fact, it seemed that his main goal in life was to avoid anything that might keep him in the same place for more than a few months. That attitude ruled out college, but left the door open for an odd sampling of jobs. For a while, it seemed as though Bob had joined the "job-of-the-month club," as he tried his hand at highway construction, photography, teaching English, and stranger careers such as meat packer, bread deliveryman, and front-door peephole salesman. Even that seemed too confining, and he headed off to Canada for a year. There he found work in a completely different field, as a music editor for a newspaper.

His newspaper experience helped him to realize that music, one of the countless subjects he had once dabbled in, was where his real interest lay. After he returned to Ireland, he and five friends decided, in 1975, to form a band. With his ability to wheel and deal, Geldof took up the job of managing the Boomtown Rats. (The Rats named themselves after a hard-luck gang in an old song by Woody Guthrie.) Managing the band wasn't enough to use up Bob's energy, though, and he took on more and more responsibility until he ended up handling the lead singing and songwriting chores as well.

Bob and the Boomtown Rats fooling around during their U.S. tour in 1979.

The Boomtown Rats tried to gain fans with some crazy tactics, such as inventing a ridiculous dance called "the Rat." But they were going nowhere in Ireland, so they took their act to England in 1976. Before long they had broken into the top forty charts with their song "Lookin' After No. 1."

No one was sure what to call their style. Some said it was punk, others insisted it was just hard rock. Whatever it was, it caught on quickly. After their single, "I Don't Like Mondays," held on to the number one spot for weeks in 1978, the group was eager for a United States tour. They hoped to make the Boomtown Rats a big name throughout the world.

That tour, however, came close to wrecking their careers. Even the praises of *Rolling Stone* magazine couldn't undo the damage of their own public relations blunders in 1979. *Rolling Stone* called Geldof "the most charismatic lead singer to emerge in Britain this decade" and applauded his singing, songwriting, and the way he handled his audiences. Although gangly and not particularly athletic, Bob reminded audiences of Mick Jagger in performing style as well as appearance. But most of the praise was buried under criticism of Geldof's rude and arrogant behavior. One of his worst moves occurred at a concert in San Diego. Geldof focused the spotlight on a group of radio executives in the audience and led the crowd in a loud chorus of booing.

After the San Diego concert, the Boomtown Rats had trouble getting their songs played on the air.

This hurt their ability to draw crowds for the rest of the tour. They returned to England, where they continued to attract enthusiastic audiences, but seemed to have lost the knack for selling records. Although their four albums found enough takers to keep them in business, they were pushed out of the top ranks of British rockers by newer, splashier groups.

By 1984, Geldof had to wonder whether it was all worth it any more. The band had no big hits out, no concert schedule to fulfill, no firm plans for the future. That left him with time on his hands. Bob Geldof left alone, free of all demands on his time, is like a nuclear reaction with all the safeguards removed. The restless energy trapped inside him had no place to vent itself. Then he happened to sit down to watch television one night, and he saw something that would change his life.

First Aid

As most of us have, Bob Geldof had seen pictures of starving people before. His reaction had been typical—the pictures had bothered him for a while, but he was able to forget about them. Perhaps, being Irish, he was affected a little more than most by the images of famine. After all, what Irishman had not heard the stories of the terrible Irish famine in 1845, in which a million out of a population of eight million had died. But Bob wasn't prepared for the horror of the documentary shown by the British Broadcasting Company on television one night in the fall of 1984. It showed the evidence of an African drought so severe that some areas hadn't had rain in three years. Thousands of people were dying, particularly in Ethiopia, and millions more faced death from starvation if something wasn't done immediately.

For once, Bob was speechless as he stared at the scenes of misery. The image that stuck in his mind was of a group of 10,000 desperately hungry people trying to divide a can of butter oil. It was decided that there was enough for 300 of them to get a taste. Geldof was struck by the quiet dignity of those who were not chosen. And he was haunted by the image of the chosen 300 going behind a wall with their meager food, so that the others wouldn't have to see them eating.

Overcome with rage and shame, Geldof sprang into action. Armed with nothing but a single argument, "why not?," he began pleading and twisting arms to get something done for the starving. Government action seemed too slow and too little, and Geldof refused to sit around helplessly while the slow wheels of government creaked into action. People were dying *now*, and he wasn't going to wait.

In his search for some way to help, Geldof became the first person to recognize the power of popular music, especially rock music. It could reach an audience and spur them into action. Along with Midge Ure of the British group Ultra Vox, Bob composed the song "Do They Know It's Christmas?" That was the easy part. The tricky part was persuading the most famous rock stars in Great Britain to give up the spotlight and

At a press conference to promote the Sport Aid benefit, Geldof played in the sand with Midge Ure, right, the musician with whom he had written "Do They Know It's Christmas?" They were joined by a friend, center, and watched by a few puzzled spectators.

donate their time to this revolutionary idea of his. As Bob later said, "Maybe I was given my arrogance and ego to do this." "Modest Bob" wasn't afraid to approach anyone, to say anything, to do anything, and to keep wearing people down with his arguments until they finally agreed. The man had once had the nerve to throw someone's "boom box" radio off a train because it was bothering him and the other passengers. Now he went after the stars with the same passionate impulse. Calling his project "Band Aid," he persuaded thirty-six British pop stars to join him. Duran Duran,

Culture Club, Sting, Wham!, Phil Collins, U2, and others all donated their services to record "Do They Know It's Christmas?" in 1984. That song became the biggest selling record in the history of Great Britain. All of the proceeds, over $14 million, went for famine relief.

Geldof's friendships with the big-name stars helped him enlist them in Band Aid. Here Bob and his girlfriend, Paula Yates, attended the premiere of a movie starring his friend Sting.

Immediately, musicians in more than twenty countries followed Geldof's cue and recorded songs to raise money for famine victims. Among those imitators was the "USA for Africa" group started by Harry Belafonte. Following the pattern set by Geldof, superstars Michael Jackson and Lionel Richie wrote the song that the group would record. Jackson, in fact, was so inspired by the idea that he sneaked into a recording studio late at night to work on "We Are The World." Sample tapes of the tune were recorded and sent off to fifty of the biggest names in United States popular music. Late in January 1985, the stars flocked to A & M recording studios in Los Angeles, California for the recording session. Bruce Springsteen, whose backing of the project guaranteed its success, flew all day after a four-hour show the night before, in order to arrive in time for the all-night recording session. Country singers such as Willie Nelson, folk heroes such as Bob Dylan and Paul Simon, veteran stars such as Ray Charles and Diana Ross, and newer acts such as Cyndi Lauper and Huey Lewis, all gathered to add their voices.

Just before the session began, Bob Geldof was introduced and received a loud round of applause from the most select musical group in the country. "The day I left Sudan was a good day," he told them. "I only saw five people die." Bob spelled out for them what the problem was; how he had seen 27,000 people trying to divide up a mere fifteen bags of flour. By the time he finished talking and telling them how they could help solve the problem, the group was more than ready to give it their best. "We Are The World" sold over a million copies in its first week.

Geldof was not content just to raise the money, however. Although he didn't think he was much of an organizer, he felt a duty to keep track of every penny of the money. After all, he had promised that one hundred percent of the money would go to the starving. People who had given the money to him trusted that he would keep his promise.

Bob's office would have made any organized businessperson gasp. The singer wasn't interested in keeping files or neat records, he just wanted to "get the stuff to Africa." He flew down to Ethiopia to see for himself what was needed. In some places there were sacks of food piled high and rotting because there was no way to get the food to the villages and camps. With that in mind, he determined that Band Aid needed to buy trucks and ships as well as food.

Bob's tireless efforts focused attention on the African famine, and he made sure he got good mileage out of the publicity. Badgering the United Nations and governments all over the world, he was able to push some of them into aiding his cause. He wasn't too proud to try *anything*: if he could get a better hearing by wearing a dreaded suit and tie, then he would put them on. Whether he was talking with Western businesspersons or Russian communists, Marxist Ethiopians or rebel armies, Geldof treated everyone the same. He didn't care who they were or what they stood for. He let them know that all he wanted to do

Bob's serious side takes over when he talks about the famine problem. He talked to the press at a conference to promote Live Aid.

was save lives, and if they wouldn't help him then they weren't any use to him.

His biggest and boldest move, however, was yet to come.

The World's Day

After "Do They Know It's Christmas?," many different countries had put out individual fund-raising records. Geldof began to dream of uniting the whole world in one giant concert to raise millions of dollars in one day.

There had been other mass rock concerts in the past, such as the Woodstock celebration sixteen years before. And there had been other mass benefit concerts, such as the Concert for Bangladesh in 1971, led by George Harrison. But what Geldof was describing was incredible. The man wanted to feature every top act he could find in a two-stage extravaganza linked by satellite and telecast to the world. One expert described it as the production nightmare of the century, but once Geldof threw himself into the project, it actually began to take shape. For six months the singer worked eighteen hours a day, seven days a week, to make his dream come true.

On July 13, 1985, the stage was set for Geldof's "global jukebox," the ultimate pop concert. More than 72,000 people crammed into London's steamy Wembley Stadium. Over 90,000 poured into JFK Stadium in Philadelphia, Pennsylvania under an equally hot sun. Backstage at these two sites, more than fifty of the top acts in popular music waited for their turns onstage. They rubbed elbows with the scores of technicians trying to pull off the most complicated telecast ever.

At Geldof's urging, some disbanded groups had agreed to get back together to help the cause. Crosby, Stills, Nash, and Young gathered for the first time in eleven years. Three-fourths of Led Zeppelin got together for the reunion. Ozzy Osbourne rejoined his old group, Black Sabbath. One of Great Britain's all-time rock favorites, The Who, had gone through a bitter break-up and had sworn never to play together again. But the fire in Geldof's voice was too moving to turn down, and The Who agreed to make up for one day.

Each group was asked to keep to a strict timetable, to play without rehearsal and without charge. For many, it meant the sacrifice of a huge payday: Hall & Oates gave up a $125,000 concert engagement.

Somehow, everything worked according to plan. An estimated 1.4 billion people from 169 countries tuned in to the giant concert. Donations flooded in at the rate of 180,000 calls per hour. Occasionally some lines of a song got lost in an electronic malfunction, but those few moments were buried in the dazzling display of talent and feeling. Elton John, Queen, and ex-Beatle Paul McCartney highlighted the British portion of the show, along with a hard-rocking performance from Geldof and his Boomtown Rats. A host of United States stars, from the queen of folk music, Joan Baez, to the "girl of the 80s," Madonna, played in Philadelphia. High-powered solo performers, most notably Mick Jagger and Tina Turner, combined their talents for special numbers. Master blues guitarist B. B. King joined the celebration, via satellite, from the Netherlands. And even though the Soviet Union did not offer a live broadcast of the concert, Geldof had included that portion of the world by booking a Russian rock band. British star Phil Collins provided the high-technology symbol for the global effort by playing in London, jetting on a supersonic transport to Philadelphia, and landing in time to lend a hand to the concert there.

In Philadelphia, more than one hundred performers gathered on stage to end the fourteen-hour show with a final chorus of "We Are The World." In London, Paul McCartney wrapped things up with an old Beatles tune, "Let It Be." While he sang, David Bowie and others hoisted Bob Geldof, clad in his usual work

Geldof at Live Aid in London. For his famine-relief efforts, he was named a Knight of the British Empire in June 1986. Because he is Irish, not British, he can't be called Sir Bob. He's just Mr. Geldof, K.B.E.

shirt, to their shoulders—in tribute to the man who made it happen.

Live Aid's success was staggering. The concert raised nearly four times what Geldof had hoped for. Other groups took note of Geldof's pioneering efforts and patterned their fund-raisers after his. Before long the

"Aid" event had become a household word. Live Aid was followed by Farm Aid, Sport Aid, Cartoon Aid, Jazz Aid, and others.

But Live Aid accomplished more than just gathering pledges of money. Equally impressive was the tremendous feeling of peace and world unity, as so many people banded together, if only for a moment, to help other people. "It was the world's day," summed up an exhausted Geldof when it was all over. He wasn't alone in believing that the world would never see a concert on that scale again.

"Halos Get Heavy And They Rust"

Along with all the money that poured in, came honors and praise for Bob Geldof. Reporters wanted to know what kind of person would give up his job for more than a year and devote so much time and energy to help people he didn't know. What was it that drove a man to such a blind commitment to a cause?

Geldof, however, shrugged off these questions as well as the nickname, "St. Bob," given to him by some of the press. "Halos get heavy and they rust," he said. It was only the fact that he wasn't anything special that had made Band Aid and Live Aid so successful, he said. If he had been more famous, professional jealousy might have prevented many stars from joining "his" show. Had he commanded a large following, governments would have been suspicious of him. Had he been in government, people wouldn't have trusted him. And if his band had been more successful, he wouldn't have had the time.

Who wouldn't get tremendous satisfaction out of raising money and then watching that money turn death into life, Geldof wanted to know. He admitted that he didn't particularly enjoy cramming his calendar with appointments and being on the phone all of the time. Bob said he wouldn't keep at it much longer. He was itching to get back to his singing career and to be able to walk, instead of run, down a street. His goal was simply to try and do his part, to save some lives, to be one of the people who tried to help when he was needed. Geldof had no illusions about being the pioneer of a new era. In fact, he predicted that his efforts had been only a moment in the sun, and that charity would probably go out of fashion in the music industry.

It would take long hours of calculation to add up Bob Geldof's share in saving lives. By the end of 1985, Band Aid alone had raised $75 million for famine relief, not only for Ethiopia, but also for Sudan, Mali, and Chad. Spin-off projects added more: USA for Africa contributed more than $42 million. Geldof's organization had purchased 200 trucks, 9 ships, and 17,000 tons of grain to stop immediate starvation. At the same time, he was looking for ways to solve the long-term problem of poverty and starvation. To that end, Band Aid contributions were building a number of villages, schools, and health centers.

Even with these accomplishments, Geldof wasn't able to win over all of his critics. Some scoffed that he was just playing the role of the concerned citizen to get publicity for his faltering Boomtown Rats. Never mind that the Rats had withdrawn their latest single, and had pushed back the release date of their latest album so people wouldn't believe that they were using the hunger issue to boost their careers. It didn't seem to matter that Geldof's time away from the group was causing financial problems for the Rats, who had to survive on money from their brief and infrequent appearances.

As Geldof resumes his career, he will probably never completely shake those critics. He hopes for another chance to write songs and to prove to the world that the Boomtown Rats really are a great band. Back in the early, successful days of the group, Geldof once commented that he felt he was born to be a rock musician. One thing is certain now. If Bob Geldof hadn't gone into music, the music world would never have come together as one to aid some dying people. And not only Africa would have been the poorer.

Photo Credits